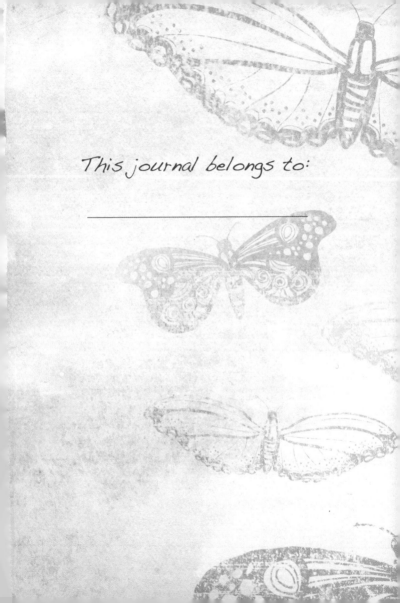

This journal belongs to:

_____

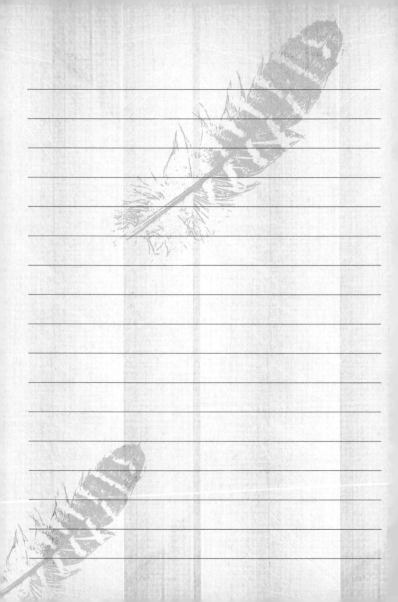

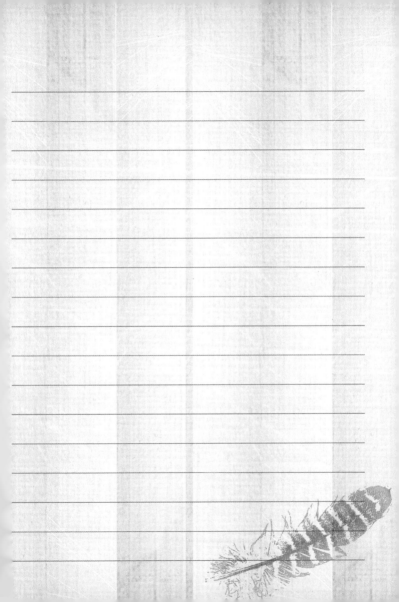

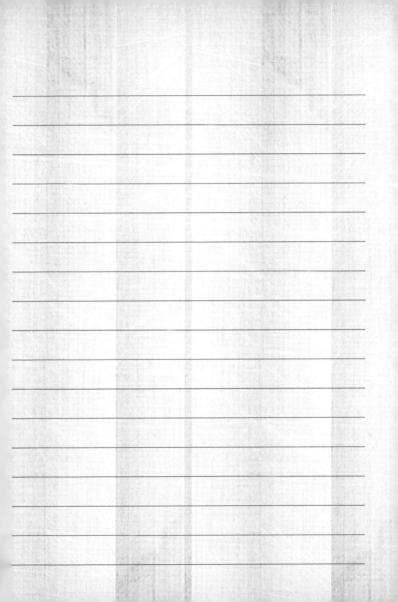

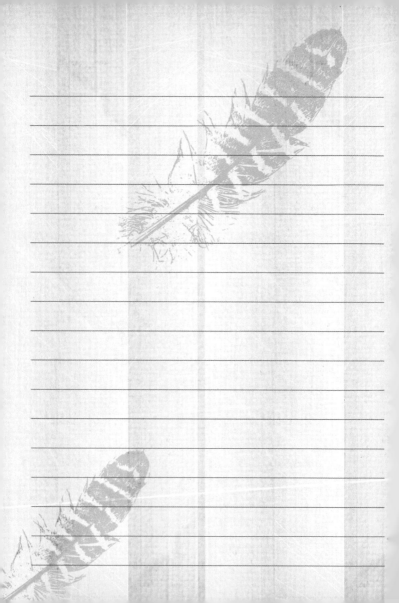

We are
shaped by
our thoughts
we become
what we think
when the
mind is
pure, joy follows
like a shadow that
never leaves.
(563 BC - 483 BC),
Buddha

We are shaped by our thoughts we become what we think when the mind is pure, joy follows like a shadow that never leaves. (563 BC - 483 BC). Buddha

joy

joy

life is like riding
a Bicycle ♡
in order to keep
your balance you
must keep moving.

Whatever you are, be a good one.

- abraham lincoln

if you do the things

you NEED

to do when you need to do them

SOMEDAY

you can do the things you

WANT to do

when you want to do them.

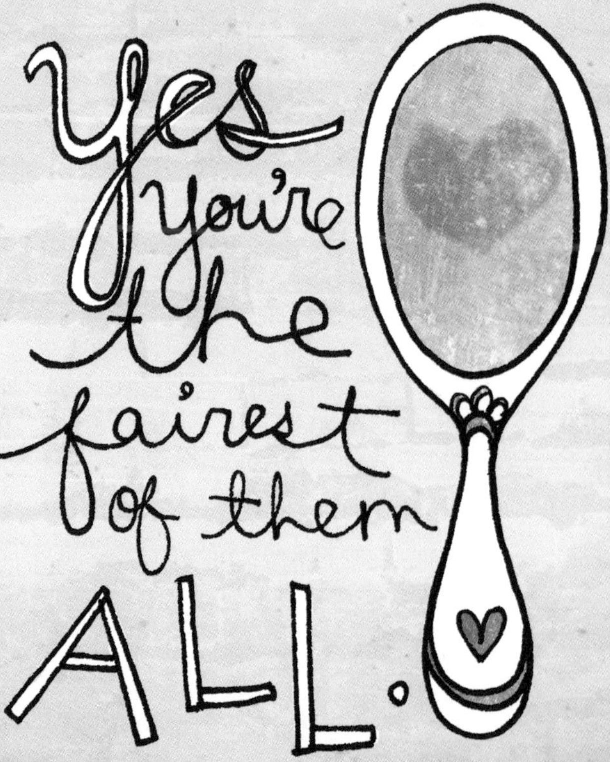
yes
you're
the
fairest
of them
ALL.

We cannot direct
THE WIND
but we can adjust
THE SAILS

What you
do, the way
you think
makes you
BEAUTIFY

BLOOM
WHERE YOU ARE
PLANTED

mary engelbreit

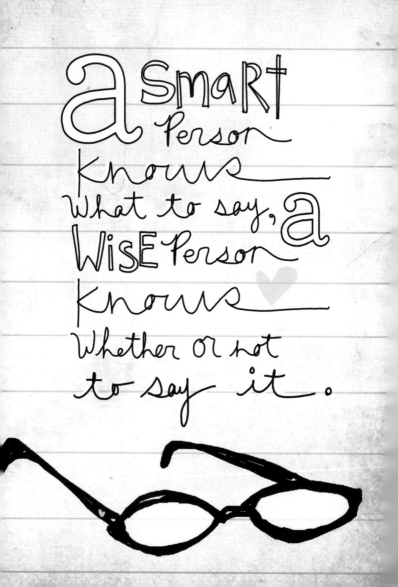

EVERY
CLOUD
has
A SiLVER
LininG.

Some See

WEEDS

others See

wishes.

THE EARTH
LAUGHS
IN FLOWERS

E.E. Cummings.

The End

Take Me With You Journal
In This Moment
208 Pages

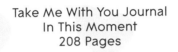

Be You.

Studio Oh!
A division of Orange Circle Studio

Irvine, CA 92618
PH: 949-727-0800
StudioOh.com

Item #80753

Printed in Korea